Making Party Decorations

Maureen Spurgeon

OXFORD
UNIVERSITY PRESS

OXFORD
UNIVERSITY PRESS

Great Clarendon Street, Oxford OX2 6DP

Oxford University Press is a department of the University of Oxford.
It furthers the University's objective of excellence in research, scholarship,
and education by publishing worldwide in

Oxford New York

Athens Auckland Bangkok Bogotá Buenos Aires Calcutta
Cape Town Chennai Dar es Salaam Delhi Florence Hong Kong Istanbul
Karachi Kuala Lumpur Madrid Melbourne Mexico City Mumbai
Nairobi Paris São Paulo Singapore Taipei Tokyo Toronto Warsaw

with associated companies in Berlin Ibadan

Oxford is a registered trade mark of Oxford University Press
in the UK and in certain other countries

Published in the United Kingdom
by Oxford University Press

Text © Maureen Spurgeon 2000

The moral rights of the author have been asserted

Database right Oxford University Press (maker)

First published 2000

British Library Cataloguing in Publication Data

Data available

ISBN 0 19 915699 9

Available in packs
Celebrations   Pack of Six (one of each book)   ISBN 0 19 915703 0
Celebrations   Class Pack (six of each book)   ISBN 0 19 915704 9

Printed in Hong Kong

Acknowledgements

All photographs are by Mark Mason.

With thanks to St Mary and John Church of England First School, Oxford.

Illustrations by Jan Lewis.

Contents

Party hats

This hat is made from a strip of card. You can decorate it in different ways, or make it into a helmet or a crown.

The basic hat

You will need

glue

a strip of corrugated card long enough to go around your head

scissors

1 Spread the glue at one end of the card. ▶

2 Stick the ends of the card together. ▼

3 Decorate your hat with paints, pencils or crayons. ▼

Other ways of decorating your hat

Cut strips of coloured paper or foil to wrap around the band.

Cut shapes from foil, wrapping paper or sweet wrappings to stick on to the band.

Stick pasta, rice or pieces of material to your hat.

Can you think of any other ways to decorate your hat?

Crown

Use foil or coloured paper shapes to make your hat into a crown.

1 Stick little pieces of foil onto card to make them stiff.

You will need

basic hat

glue

foil

card

straws

scissors

2 Cut out pairs of shapes and stick them on lengths of straw.

3 Glue the straws and slide them into the rim of the hat.

4 Stick more shapes around the hat.

Soldier's helmet

Use more strips of card to make your hat into a soldier's helmet.

1 Stick the card strips on foil and cut off any extra foil.

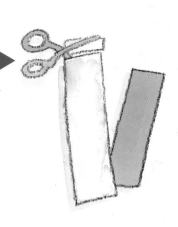

You will need

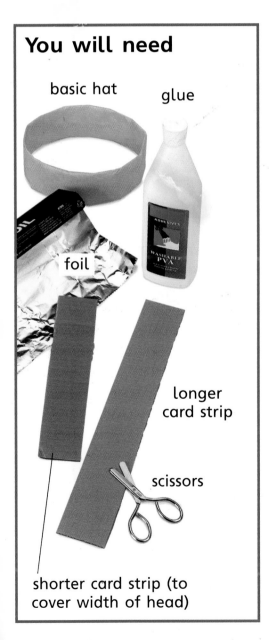

basic hat

glue

foil

longer card strip

scissors

shorter card strip (to cover width of head)

2 Cut the end of the long strip into a point.

3 Glue the middle of the short strip of foil and stick the long strip across it.

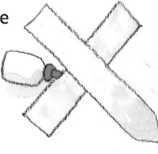

4 Stick the pointed end to the front of the hat. Stick the other ends to the back and sides of the hat.

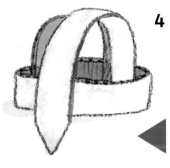

Piñatas

A piñata is filled with sweets and presents. It is hung up and people take it in turns to hit the piñata until it breaks open and the treats fall out. Piñatas are traditional New Year decorations in Mexico, but they are fun at any time of the year.

For the piñata shape

You will need

old newspaper

long piece of string

balloon

scissors

flour and water paste

1 Blow up the balloon and knot it firmly. Tie string around the knotted end.

2 Mix one part of flour to two parts of water to make the paste.

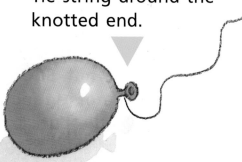

3 Tear newspaper into small pieces. Dip the pieces in a saucer of cold water. ▼

4 Brush paste on the balloon and stick on pieces of newspaper. ▼

5 Turn it upside down to finish covering it. ▼

Cover the balloon with four or five layers of paste and newspaper pieces. Leave it for at least a day to dry and harden.

6 Burst the balloon with a pin. Slit the piñata, and put sweets and presents inside. ▼

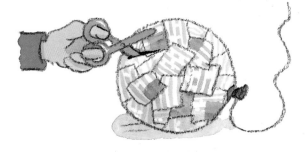

7 Seal the hole with sticky tape. ▼

Decorating your piñata

You will need

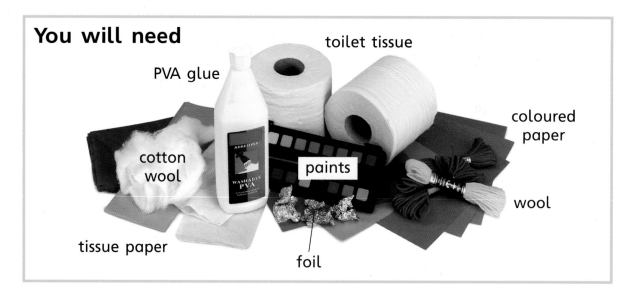

PVA glue

toilet tissue

cotton wool

paints

coloured paper

wool

tissue paper

foil

Funny face

1 Make a funny face on your piñata. ▼

2 Dab glue on the top of the piñata and stick on some wool, paper loops, or cotton wool to make hair. ▶

3 Cut out shapes for hands and feet, and stick on. ▶

Bird piñata

1 Cut out paper or foil shapes for your bird.

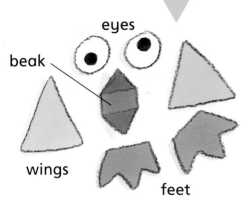

eyes

beak

wings

feet

2 Stick the shapes on the body of the piñata with glue.

3 Cut pieces of tissue paper into feather shapes.

4 Use glue to stick the top of each feather piece to the piñata.

Rangoli patterns

In India, rangoli patterns are made on the ground outside as decorations for people's homes. Rangoli patterns on round pieces of card can be put anywhere.

For a colour rangoli

You will need

modelling clay

coloured crêpe paper

card

saucer half full of water

scissors

pencil

1 Draw around a large dinner plate on the card. Cut out the circle.

2 Roll the modelling clay into balls or long, thin sausages.

3 Lay the clay on the card to make a pattern.

4 Crumple a small piece of crêpe paper and dip the tip in water.

5 Dab the damp crêpe paper around the clay. Leave the board to dry.

6 Peel away the clay to see the rangoli pattern.

A two-colour rangoli pattern

1 Lay the clay pieces on the card again.

2 Dab with damp crêpe paper of another colour and leave to dry. Peel away the clay, as before.

Using seeds

You will need

glue

card circle

paint

pasta shapes

seeds (dry them first on newspaper)

1 Add a few drops of paint to the glue, then brush it on to the card.

2 Stick a large dried pea, or piece of pasta in the centre of the card. Then arrange the seeds into a pattern, spreading out from the centre.

3 Fill spaces in the rangoli pattern with small seeds.

Using paper

You will need

card circle

sweet wrappings

foil

strips and pieces of tissue

glue

1 Draw a pattern on the card. ▶

2 Cut tissue into thin strips. Then, glue a strip of tissue around the edge. Push it along with a blunt pencil to make it into folds. ▼

3 Make rangoli flowers by twisting the ends of smaller pieces of tissue. ▼

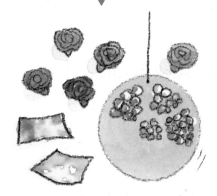

4 Add sparkle using crumpled sweet wrappings and pieces of foil.

15

Banners

You can make a **banner** for a birthday party with squares of card.

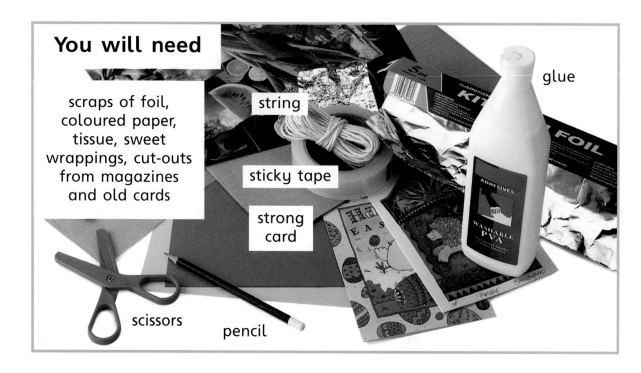

You will need

scraps of foil, coloured paper, tissue, sweet wrappings, cut-outs from magazines and old cards

string

sticky tape

strong card

glue

scissors

pencil

1 Draw the outline of the letters you want to use on each square.

2 Brush glue on each letter.

3 Stick on bits of foil, tissue, coloured paper scraps and cut-out pictures.

4 Ask an adult to help you make holes at each corner of the squares.

5 Thread one string through the top holes and one string through the bottom holes. Tie knots at the ends.

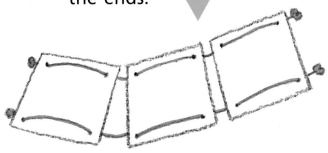

6 Tape the string to the back of each card to stop it sliding.

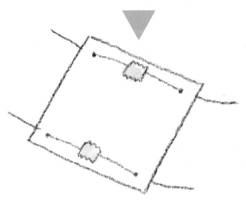

Mendhi

In many Asian countries, people decorate their hands and feet with mendhi designs for special occasions.
You can make mendhi decorations on card.

You will need

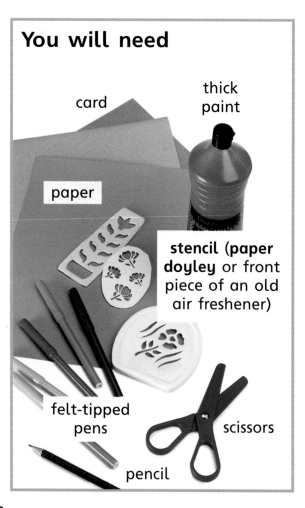

card

thick paint

paper

stencil (**paper doyley** or front piece of an old air freshener)

felt-tipped pens

scissors

pencil

1 Put your hand on the card and draw round it.

2 Cut out the hand-shape to make a template.

3 Place the template on paper, draw round it and cut out.

4 Lay a **stencil** on the hand shape. Using felt-tipped pens, colour through the holes on to the paper. Use brown paint to make a henna-coloured pattern. ▼

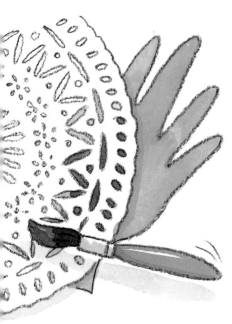

5 Lift the stencil carefully. ▼

6 Thread the mendhi designs on a string or glue them on a large piece of paper or card. ▼

Mendhi streamers

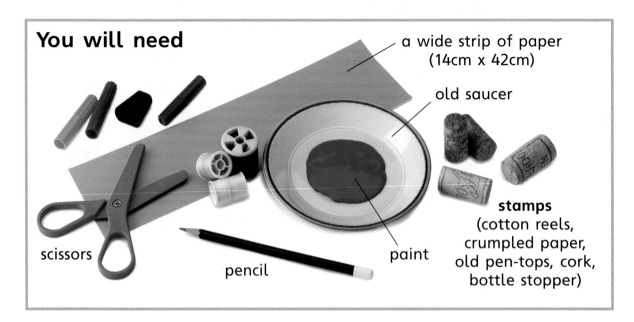

a wide strip of paper
(14cm x 42cm)

old saucer

stamps
(cotton reels,
crumpled paper,
old pen-tops, cork,
bottle stopper)

scissors

pencil

paint

1 Fold the paper into a
pad by folding it one
way and then the other.
Draw a hand shape on
top. The edge of the
thumb and little finger
must touch the folded
edges of the pad.

2 Cut out the hand shape,
except for the side of the
thumb and little finger.

3 Unfold the paper strip.

20

4 Pour some paint into an old saucer. Dip a **stamp** into the paint.

5 Press the stamp on the hand shapes.

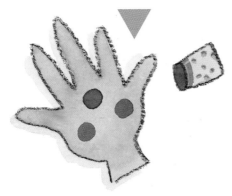

6 Use different stamps and colours to complete the pattern.

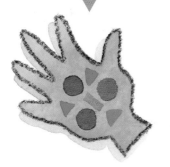

Foot designs

Use a card sole as a pattern, instead of your hand. Remember that the edge of each foot shape must touch the folded edges of the paper, to make a streamer.

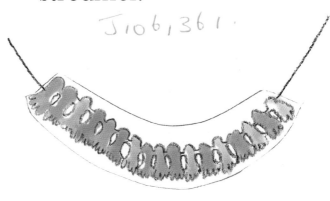

Flowers

Plastic flowers can be tied in bunches or threaded on string to make a hanging decoration.

You will need

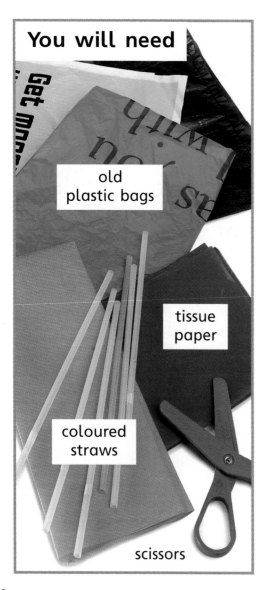

old plastic bags

tissue paper

coloured straws

scissors

1 Cut the handles and bottom off the plastic bags and cut into squares.

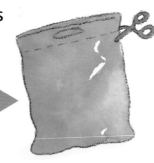

2 Fold the squares into quarters. Snip the tip off the folded corner.

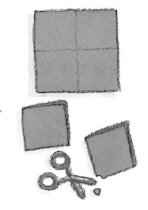

3 Cut the open (unfolded) sides into a curved shape and cut a zig-zagged, frilly or fringed border.

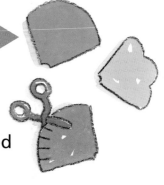

4 Open out the flower.

5 Make more flower pieces, with different edges. Thread them on to the top end of a drinking straw. ▼

6 Make four cuts in the top of the drinking straw. ▼

7 Bend the four strips back and fill the straw hole with tissue. ▼

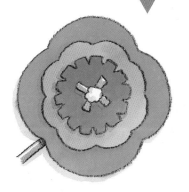

8 Five different coloured flowers make a pretty bunch. ▼

To make a garland

Put flowers on short lengths of straw and thread them on to a piece of string.

Glossary

banner A piece of cloth or paper with a message on it that can be hung up or carried.

garland A circle of flowers.

paper doyley A decorative piece of paper often put under cakes.

stamp A tool for printing

stencil A piece of material or card with patterns cut out for making patterns.

Index